CONTENTS

INTRODUCTION

Welcome to the exciting world of building your own gaming PC! In this comprehensive guide, we will embark on a journey together to demystify the process of assembling a powerful and customized gaming rig. Whether you're a seasoned gamer seeking to elevate your gaming experience or a curious enthusiast ready to dive into the world of PC building, this book will equip you with the knowledge and confidence to create a gaming setup that exceeds your expectations.

In an era where gaming technology advances at a rapid pace, building your own PC has become more accessible than ever before. Gone are the days of settling for pre-built systems with limited upgrade options. By taking control of the building process, you open up a realm of possibilities where every component, from the graphics card to the cooling system, is handpicked to suit your specific needs and desires.

Throughout these pages, we will explore the essential components that make up a gaming PC, unravel the mysteries of compatibility and performance optimization, and guide you through the step-by-step process of putting it all together. From selecting the perfect processor to understanding the intricacies of RAM and storage options, we'll cover it all.

But building a gaming PC is not just about technical details

—it's about unleashing your creativity and personalizing a system that reflects your unique style. We'll delve into the world of aesthetics, exploring stunning case designs, RGB lighting options, and cable management techniques that will make your PC a work of art.

Moreover, we'll navigate the ever-changing landscape of gaming hardware, discussing emerging technologies, trends, and the considerations you need to keep in mind for future-proofing your system. From virtual reality and ray tracing to overclocking and cooling solutions, you'll gain the knowledge to stay at the forefront of gaming innovation.

So, whether you're a newcomer to the world of PC building or an experienced enthusiast looking to upgrade, this book will serve as your trusted companion. Get ready to embark on a thrilling adventure that will empower you to create a gaming PC that not only meets but surpasses your expectations. Let's dive in and unlock the true potential of your gaming experience!

CHAPTER ONE

Introduction to PC Gaming

The Rise of PC Gaming

PC gaming has witnessed a remarkable rise in popularity over the years. With advancements in technology and the increasing demand for immersive gaming experiences, the gaming industry has seen a significant shift towards PC gaming. Several factors have contributed to this rise, including the availability of powerful hardware, diverse gaming options, and the growth of online gaming communities.

One of the key reasons for the rise of PC gaming is the continuous improvement of hardware components. Graphics cards, processors, and memory modules have become more powerful and affordable, allowing gamers to enjoy high-quality visuals and smooth gameplay. Moreover, the constant innovation in PC hardware has enabled developers to create visually stunning and resource-intensive games that were once exclusive to consoles.

Another factor that has contributed to the popularity of PC gaming is the wide variety of gaming options available. Unlike consoles, which are limited to a specific set of games, PC gamers have access to a vast library of titles from various genres. From massive multiplayer online games to indie masterpieces, the PC gaming market offers something for every type of gamer. This diverse selection of games has attracted a large and dedicated community of players, further fueling the rise of PC gaming.

The rise of online gaming communities has also played a significant role in the popularity of PC gaming. Through platforms such as Steam, Discord, and Twitch, gamers can connect with fellow players, share experiences, and participate in multiplayer matches. These communities provide a sense of belonging and foster social interactions among gamers, making the PC gaming experience more engaging and enjoyable.

Additionally, the flexibility and customization options offered by PC gaming have attracted many enthusiasts. Building a gaming PC allows players to personalize their setups according to their preferences and budget. From choosing specific components to creating unique aesthetics with RGB lighting and custom cases, PC gamers have the freedom to create a gaming rig that reflects their individual style. This level of customization enhances the overall gaming experience and fosters a sense of ownership and pride among PC gamers.

In recent years, the rise of esports has further propelled the growth of PC gaming. Competitive gaming tournaments and leagues have gained significant traction, with professional players and teams competing for lucrative prizes. The accessibility of PC gaming, along with the ability to achieve high frame rates and low input lag, has made it the platform of choice for competitive gaming. As a result, PC gaming has become synonymous with esports, attracting a large viewer base and driving further interest in the gaming community.

To summarize, the rise of PC gaming can be attributed to various factors, including advancements in hardware technology, a diverse selection of games, the growth of online gaming communities, the flexibility of customization, and the prominence of esports. As the gaming industry continues to evolve, PC gaming is expected to maintain its popularity and further push the boundaries of immersive gaming experiences.

Benefits of Building Your Own Gaming PC

Building your own gaming PC offers a multitude of benefits that go beyond simply having a powerful gaming rig. From cost savings to customization options, building a gaming PC allows you to create a personalized setup tailored to your specific needs and preferences. Let's explore some of the key advantages of building your own gaming PC.

- Cost-effectiveness: Building your own gaming PC can often be more cost-effective compared to buying a pre-built system. By carefully selecting individual components, you have the flexibility to prioritize your budget on the most important aspects, such as the graphics card and processor, while making cost-efficient choices for other components. This way, you can optimize the performance-to-price ratio and potentially save money compared to purchasing a pre-built PC.
- Customization: One of the most significant advantages of building a gaming PC is the ability to customize every aspect of your setup. From choosing the case design and RGB lighting to selecting specific hardware components, you have

full control over the aesthetics and functionality of your PC. This level of customization allows you to create a unique gaming rig that reflects your personal style and preferences.

- Performance optimization: Building your own gaming PC enables you to fine-tune the performance based on your gaming requirements. You can select components that best suit your needs, whether you prioritize high-resolution gaming, competitive esports, or content creation. This customization allows you to achieve the desired balance between graphics quality, processing power, and storage capacity, ensuring an optimal gaming experience.

- Upgradability: Gaming PCs are not static systems; they can be upgraded over time to keep up with the latest technologies and gaming demands. By building your own PC, you have a better understanding of its internal components and can easily upgrade specific parts as needed. This upgradability gives you the flexibility to stay at the cutting edge of gaming technology without having to replace the entire system.

- Learning experience: Building a gaming PC is an educational and rewarding experience. It provides an opportunity to learn about computer hardware, gain hands-on experience in assembling components, and troubleshoot any issues that may arise. This knowledge can be valuable in the long run, as you develop a better understanding of how your gaming PC works and can perform basic maintenance and upgrades without relying on external assistance.

- Community and support: The PC building community is vast and supportive, with numerous online forums, tutorials, and resources available to assist beginners and experienced builders alike. Engaging with this community can provide valuable insights, tips, and troubleshooting assistance throughout the building process. Additionally, being part of this community allows you to share your experiences, seek advice, and contribute to the collective knowledge of PC enthusiasts.

In conclusion, building your own gaming PC offers several benefits, including cost-effectiveness, customization options, performance optimization, upgradability, and a valuable learning experience. By taking the time to research, select components, and assemble your PC, you can create a gaming rig that not only meets your gaming needs but also provides a sense of ownership and pride in your setup.

Understanding Gaming PC Components

To build a gaming PC or make informed decisions about upgrading your existing setup, it is essential to have a good understanding of the various components that make up a gaming PC. Here, we will explore the key components involved in a gaming PC and their roles in delivering optimal gaming performance.

- Central Processing Unit (CPU): The CPU is often referred to as the "brain" of a computer. It handles the majority of calculations and instructions necessary for running applications and games. In gaming, the CPU's performance is crucial for tasks such as physics simulations, artificial intelligence, and overall game optimization. When choosing a CPU, factors to consider include clock speed, core count, and architecture.

- Graphics Processing Unit (GPU): The GPU, also known as the graphics card, is responsible for rendering images and videos on your monitor. It is a vital component for gaming, as it determines the visual quality, frame rates, and overall smoothness of gameplay. When selecting a GPU, factors to consider include memory capacity, CUDA cores (for NVIDIA GPUs), and clock speeds. High-end GPUs are typically recommended for gamers aiming for high-resolution gaming or virtual reality experiences.

- Random Access Memory (RAM): RAM is the temporary storage space used by the CPU to hold data that is actively being processed. In gaming, having sufficient RAM is crucial for smooth gameplay, as it affects the loading times, multitasking ability, and overall performance of games. When choosing RAM, factors to consider include capacity (measured in gigabytes) and speed (measured in megahertz).

- Storage: Gaming PCs typically utilize two types of storage: solid-state drives (SSDs) and hard disk drives (HDDs). SSDs offer faster data access speeds, resulting in quicker game loading times and improved system responsiveness. HDDs, on the other hand, provide higher storage capacity at a more affordable price per gigabyte. Many gamers opt for a combination of both, using an SSD for the operating system and frequently played games, while utilizing an HDD for mass storage.

- Motherboard: The motherboard serves as the main circuit board that connects all the components of a gaming PC. It houses the CPU, GPU, RAM, storage drives, and other peripherals. When selecting a motherboard, it is crucial to ensure compatibility with the CPU and other components, as well as considering the available expansion slots, connectivity options, and overall build quality.
- Power Supply Unit (PSU): The PSU is responsible for supplying power to all the components in the PC. It is essential to choose a PSU with sufficient wattage to support the power requirements of the CPU, GPU, and other components. Additionally, considering factors such as efficiency rating, modular or non-modular design, and brand reliability is crucial to ensure stable power delivery and long-term reliability.
- Cooling: Adequate cooling is essential to prevent overheating and maintain optimal performance. This can be achieved through various cooling solutions, including air cooling (using fans and heatsinks) or liquid cooling (utilizing a liquid coolant and radiators). Ensuring proper airflow within the PC case and selecting appropriate cooling components is crucial for maintaining stable temperatures during intense gaming sessions.

It is important to note that the above components are just the core elements of a gaming PC. Additional peripherals such as monitors, keyboards, mice, and audio equipment also play a significant role in enhancing the gaming experience.

By understanding the roles and specifications of these gaming PC components, you can make informed decisions when selecting and upgrading your hardware. This knowledge empowers you to create a well-balanced gaming PC that meets your specific requirements and ensures an immersive and enjoyable gaming experience.

Understanding Hardware Components

Central Processing Unit (CPU)

The Central Processing Unit (CPU) is often considered the "brain" of a computer. It is responsible for executing instructions, performing calculations, and managing data processing. When it comes to gaming, the CPU plays a crucial role in handling tasks such as physics simulations, artificial intelligence, and overall game optimization.

When selecting a CPU for gaming, several factors need to be considered. One of the key factors is the clock speed, which determines how many instructions the CPU can execute per second. Higher clock speeds generally result in faster processing and better gaming performance. However, it's important to strike a balance between clock speed and the number of cores. Modern CPUs often come with multiple cores, allowing for better multitasking and improved performance in games that utilize multiple threads.

Another consideration is the CPU architecture. Different generations and models of CPUs may have varying architectures, which can impact performance. It's worth researching benchmarks and reviews to determine which CPUs offer the best performance for gaming within your budget.

Graphics Processing Unit (GPU)

The Graphics Processing Unit (GPU), also known as the graphics card, is a critical component for gaming. The GPU is responsible for rendering images, videos, and animations, delivering the visual quality and frame rates in games.

When it comes to gaming, the GPU's performance is crucial. Higher-end GPUs are often recommended for gamers who want to experience high-resolution gaming or virtual reality. GPUs are equipped with dedicated memory (VRAM) to store and process the graphical data required for rendering. The amount of VRAM can impact the GPU's ability to handle higher resolutions and more detailed textures.

Factors to consider when selecting a GPU include memory capacity, CUDA cores (for NVIDIA GPUs), clock speeds, and cooling solutions. It's also essential to ensure compatibility with your monitor's resolution and refresh rate to make the most out of your gaming experience.

Random Access Memory (RAM)

Random Access Memory (RAM) is temporary storage that the CPU uses to hold data that is actively being processed. In gaming, having sufficient RAM is crucial for smooth gameplay, as it affects loading times, multitasking ability, and overall performance.

When choosing RAM for a gaming PC, the capacity and speed are important factors to consider. The capacity of RAM is measured in gigabytes (GB), and it's recommended to have at least 8GB for most modern games. However, for smoother performance and future-proofing, opting for 16GB or even 32GB may be beneficial.

RAM speed, measured in megahertz (MHz), determines how quickly data can be read from or written to RAM. Higher RAM speeds can provide a slight performance boost, especially in CPU-intensive games. However, the actual impact on gaming performance is usually not as significant as other components like the CPU and GPU.

THE ULTIMATE GAMING PC BUILDING GUIDE

Storage Options (HDD, SSD, NVMe)

Storage options for gaming PCs typically include Hard Disk Drives (HDDs), Solid-State Drives (SSDs), and NVMe (Non-Volatile Memory Express) drives.

HDDs are traditional storage devices that offer higher capacity at a more affordable price per gigabyte. They are suitable for storing large game libraries and multimedia files. However, HDDs have slower data access speeds compared to SSDs and NVMe drives, resulting in longer loading times.

SSDs provide faster data access speeds, resulting in quicker game loading times and improved system responsiveness. They are more expensive per gigabyte compared to HDDs but offer a significant improvement in overall performance.

NVMe drives utilize the NVMe interface and provide even faster data transfer speeds than traditional SSDs. They offer the fastest storage solution for gaming PCs, significantly reducing game loading times and file transfer speeds. However, NVMe drives tend to be more expensive than both HDDs and SSDs.

Many gamers opt for a combination of storage options. For example, using an SSD for the operating system and frequently played games, while utilizing an HDD for mass storage of less frequently accessed games and media files.

Motherboard and Expansion Slots

The motherboard is the main circuit board that connects all the components in a gaming PC. It serves as a central hub, providing power, data connectivity, and expansion slots for additional components.

When selecting a motherboard, it's crucial to ensure compatibility with the CPU and other components. Consider the socket type, which determines the CPU models that can be installed. Additionally, check the chipset, as different chipsets may offer varying features and performance levels.

Expansion slots on the motherboard allow for future upgrades and additions to the gaming PC. Common expansion slots include PCIe (Peripheral Component Interconnect Express) slots for installing additional GPUs, sound cards, or high-speed storage drives. It's important to consider the number and types of expansion slots available on the motherboard based on your potential upgrade needs.

Other factors to consider when selecting a motherboard include the number of RAM slots, the availability of USB ports, connectivity options (such as Wi-Fi and Bluetooth), and the overall build quality and reliability of the motherboard manufacturer.

Power Supply Unit (PSU)

The Power Supply Unit (PSU) is responsible for supplying power to all the components in a gaming PC. It's crucial to choose a PSU with sufficient wattage to support the power requirements of the CPU, GPU, and other components.

When selecting a PSU, consider the total power consumption of your system, factoring in the power requirements of the CPU and GPU under maximum load. It's recommended to have some headroom to account for potential upgrades or additions to the system in the future.

Other factors to consider when choosing a PSU include efficiency rating (such as 80 Plus certification), modular or non-modular design, and brand reliability. Higher efficiency PSUs waste less energy, resulting in reduced heat output and potentially lower energy bills.

Cooling Solutions (Air vs. Liquid)

Proper cooling is crucial for maintaining optimal performance and preventing overheating in a gaming PC. There are two primary cooling solutions: air cooling and liquid cooling.

Air cooling involves using fans and heatsinks to dissipate heat from the CPU, GPU, and other components. It is the most common cooling solution and is generally more affordable and easier to install. Proper airflow within the PC case, achieved by strategically placing fans, is crucial for effective air cooling.

Liquid cooling, also known as water cooling, utilizes a liquid coolant and a radiator to dissipate heat from the components. It provides more efficient heat transfer and can result in lower temperatures compared to air cooling. Liquid cooling is often used by enthusiasts and overclockers who aim to push their components to their limits. However, liquid cooling can be more expensive and complex to install and maintain compared to air cooling.

The choice between air cooling and liquid cooling depends on personal preference, budget, and the level of overclocking or system optimization you plan to undertake.

Peripherals and Accessories

Peripherals and accessories play an important role in enhancing the gaming experience. These include monitors, keyboards, mice, audio equipment, and other devices.

When selecting a gaming monitor, consider factors such as resolution, refresh rate, response time, and panel type. Higher resolutions, such as 1440p or 4K, offer sharper and more detailed visuals. Higher refresh rates, such as 144Hz or 240Hz, provide smoother motion and reduced motion blur. Response time affects how quickly pixels can change colors, impacting the visual clarity in fast-paced games. Panel types, such as TN, IPS, or VA, have different characteristics in terms of color accuracy, viewing angles, and contrast ratios.

For gaming keyboards and mice, consider factors such as mechanical or membrane switches, programmable keys, customization options, and ergonomic design. Mechanical keyboards offer a more tactile and responsive typing experience, while gaming mice often feature higher DPI (dots per inch) for precise tracking and programmable buttons for customization.

Audio equipment, such as headphones or speakers, can enhance the immersive experience of gaming. Consider features such as surround sound, frequency response, and comfort for extended gaming sessions.

Other accessories that can enhance the gaming experience include gaming controllers, mousepads, gaming chairs, and RGB lighting solutions. These accessories provide additional comfort, control, and customization options based on personal preferences.

In conclusion, understanding the components of a gaming PC is crucial for building or upgrading a system that meets your gaming needs. By considering the CPU, GPU, RAM, storage options, motherboard, PSU, cooling solutions, and peripherals, you can create a well-balanced gaming setup that delivers optimal performance and an immersive gaming experience.

Setting A Budget And Choosing Your Components

Determining Your Gaming Needs

Before building a gaming PC, it's important to determine your gaming needs and goals. Consider the types of games you play or intend to play, the desired graphical settings and resolutions, and any specific requirements for multiplayer or competitive gaming. This will help you understand the level of performance and hardware specifications you should aim for.

For example, if you primarily play less demanding games or older titles, you may not need a high-end GPU or the latest CPU. On the other hand, if you're interested in playing graphically demanding games at 4K resolution or VR experiences, you'll need more powerful components to achieve smooth gameplay.

Additionally, consider if you have any non-gaming requirements, such as content creation or streaming. These tasks may require more processing power or additional RAM.

Balancing Performance and Cost

Building a gaming PC involves finding a balance between performance and cost. While it's tempting to opt for the latest and most powerful components, it's essential to consider your budget and prioritize the components that have the most significant impact on gaming performance.

Typically, the GPU and CPU have the most significant influence on gaming performance. Allocating a higher portion of your budget to these components can result in a more significant improvement in gaming experience. However, it's important to avoid overspending on components that may not provide noticeable benefits for your specific gaming needs.

Consider the trade-offs between cost and performance when selecting other components, such as RAM, storage options, and cooling solutions. You may be able to save money by choosing a slightly lower capacity of RAM or opting for a combination of HDD and SSD storage instead of going all-in on high-capacity SSDs.

Researching and Selecting Components

Thorough research is crucial when selecting components for your gaming PC. Read reviews, benchmarks, and comparisons of different models to understand their performance, reliability, and value for money.

Websites, forums, and communities dedicated to PC building and gaming can provide valuable insights and recommendations. Engage with these resources to gather information, ask questions, and seek advice from experienced builders and gamers.

Consider the specific features, specifications, and compatibility of each component. Compare options from different brands and models to find the best fit for your requirements and budget.

Additionally, consider the warranties and after-sales support offered by manufacturers. Reliable customer support and warranty coverage can provide peace of mind and assistance in case of any issues with the components.

Compatibility Considerations

Compatibility is a crucial factor when selecting components for your gaming PC. Ensure that all components are compatible with each other and with your intended use.

Check the socket compatibility between the CPU and motherboard to ensure they can work together. Additionally, verify the RAM compatibility with the motherboard, such as the supported speed and capacity.

Pay attention to the power requirements of the components and ensure that the PSU can provide sufficient power and connectors to support them. Confirm that the GPU length and dimensions fit within the available space in your PC case.

It's also important to consider the connectivity options of the motherboard, such as the number of USB ports, audio jacks, and expansion slots, to accommodate your peripherals and future upgrade plans.

To simplify the compatibility checking process, online tools and PC building guides can help you ensure that the selected components are compatible with each other.

In conclusion, determining your gaming needs, balancing performance and cost, thorough research, and considering compatibility are crucial steps in selecting the right components for your gaming PC. By carefully considering these factors, you can build a system that meets your gaming requirements and provides an enjoyable gaming experience.

CHAPTER TWO

Building Your Gaming PC

Preparing the Workspace and Tools

Before starting the assembly process, it's important to prepare your workspace and gather the necessary tools. Here are some steps to follow:

- Choose a clean, well-lit area with a sturdy table or workbench. Ensure you have enough space to comfortably assemble the PC and access all components.
- Gather the necessary tools, which typically include a screwdriver (preferably magnetic), thermal paste (if not pre-applied on the CPU cooler), cable ties or Velcro straps for cable management, and an anti-static wrist strap (optional but recommended to prevent electrostatic discharge).
- Remove any static-inducing materials from your workspace, such as carpets or rugs, to reduce the risk of damaging sensitive components with static electricity.
- Organize your components, manuals, and screws in separate containers or trays to keep them easily accessible during the assembly process.
- Ensure you have a stable internet connection to

download drivers or updates for your components after assembly.

Step-by-Step Assembly Process

The following steps provide a general overview of the assembly process for a gaming PC. Refer to the specific manuals and instructions provided with your components for detailed guidance.

- Start by mounting the CPU and cooler onto the motherboard. Remove the CPU socket cover, gently align the CPU with the socket, and secure it in place. Apply thermal paste (if necessary) and attach the cooler according to the manufacturer's instructions.
- Install the motherboard into the PC case. Line up the motherboard's I/O shield with the corresponding cutout on the case. Carefully place the motherboard onto the standoffs and secure it with screws, ensuring it is securely and evenly mounted.
- Install the RAM modules into the motherboard's memory slots. Align the notch on the RAM module with the corresponding slot on the motherboard and firmly press down until it clicks into place. Make sure the retaining clips on both sides lock the RAM in place.
- Install storage devices, such as SSDs or HDDs, into the appropriate drive bays or slots in the case. Secure them using screws or brackets provided. Connect the necessary data cables (SATA or M.2) to the storage devices and the motherboard.
- Connect the power supply to the motherboard and

other components. Plug in the necessary power cables, including the 24-pin ATX power connector, CPU power connector, and PCIe power connectors for the GPU. Ensure all connections are secure.

- Install the GPU into the appropriate PCIe slot on the motherboard. Align the GPU with the slot and firmly push it down until it is fully seated. Secure the GPU to the case using screws or brackets if required. Connect the necessary power cables from the PSU to the GPU.

- Connect all other necessary cables, such as SATA data and power cables for storage devices, case fans, USB headers, and audio connectors. Ensure cables are neatly routed and organized for optimal airflow and aesthetics.

- Double-check all connections and make sure everything is securely fastened. Close the PC case and secure it with screws.

Installing the CPU and Cooler

Remove the CPU socket cover on the motherboard, usually by gently lifting a lever or latch.

- Carefully align the CPU with the socket, ensuring the orientation is correct (refer to the CPU and motherboard manuals for guidance).

- Gently place the CPU into the socket, ensuring all pins or contacts align properly. Avoid applying excessive force or wiggling the CPU.

- Once the CPU is properly aligned, lower the socket lever or latch to secure the CPU in place.

- If the CPU cooler requires thermal paste, apply a small, pea-sized amount onto the center of the

CPU.

- Attach the CPU cooler to the motherboard, following the manufacturer's instructions. This may involve aligning mounting brackets, applying pressure, or securing screws or clips.

Mounting the Motherboard

- Remove the I/O shield that came with the motherboard from its packaging.
- Align the I/O shield with the corresponding cutout on the back of the PC case. Gently press it into place until it fits securely.
- Carefully lower the motherboard onto the standoffs inside the case, ensuring the I/O ports align with the I/O shield.
- Insert screws through the motherboard mounting holes into the standoffs. Tighten the screws evenly, alternating between them, until the motherboard is securely attached to the case.

Installing RAM and Storage Devices

- Locate the RAM slots on the motherboard. Refer to the motherboard manual to identify the correct slots for the number of RAM modules you have.
- Gently press the RAM modules into the slots, ensuring they are aligned properly. Apply even pressure until the module clicks into place and the retaining clips on both sides lock the RAM.
- For storage devices, determine the appropriate drive bays or slots in the case.
- For SSDs or HDDs, secure them in the designated drive bays using screws or brackets provided.

Ensure they are firmly attached to prevent movement.

- Connect the necessary data cables (SATA or M.2) from the storage devices to the corresponding ports on the motherboard.

Connecting Power Supply and Cables

- Identify the necessary power cables for the motherboard, CPU, and GPU.
- Connect the 24-pin ATX power connector from the power supply to the corresponding port on the motherboard.
- Connect the CPU power connector from the power supply to the appropriate port on the motherboard. This is typically an 8-pin or 4-pin connector near the CPU socket.
- Connect PCIe power connectors from the power supply to the GPU, if required. Refer to the GPU manual for the specific power requirements.
- Connect SATA power cables from the power supply to the storage devices, providing power for their operation.
- Connect any additional power cables required for case fans, RGB lighting, or other components.

Installing the GPU and Expansion Cards

- Identify the appropriate PCIe slot for the GPU on the motherboard. It is typically the topmost full-length slot.
- Remove the expansion slot covers on the back of the PC case to accommodate the GPU.
- Align the GPU with the PCIe slot and gently press

it into place. Ensure it is fully seated and the locking mechanism clicks into place.

- Secure the GPU to the case using screws or brackets, if provided.
- Connect the necessary power cables from the power supply to the GPU. This may involve one or more PCIe power connectors.
- If installing other expansion cards, such as sound cards or Wi-Fi cards, follow the manufacturer's instructions and insert them into the appropriate PCIe slots on the motherboard. Secure them with screws or brackets if required.

Cable Management Techniques

Effective cable management helps improve airflow, optimize cooling, and create a cleaner aesthetic. Here are some cable management techniques:

- Use cable ties or Velcro straps to group and secure cables together, keeping them organized and preventing them from obstructing airflow.
- Route cables behind the motherboard tray or along designated cable management channels to keep them out of sight and improve airflow.
- Leave enough slack in the cables to allow for future component upgrades or repositioning.
- Bundle excess cables and tuck them away in unused drive bays or designated cable management areas in the case.
- Consider using cable combs or sleeves to further neaten and organize cables.

Testing and Troubleshooting

After assembling the PC, it's important to test its functionality and address any potential issues. Follow these steps:

- Connect the PC to a power source and ensure the power supply switch is in the "on" position.
- Press the power button on the PC case to turn on the system. Verify that all fans are spinning, including the CPU and GPU fans.
- Check if the motherboard LEDs or debug indicators display any error codes or warnings. Refer to the motherboard manual for troubleshooting steps if necessary.
- Enter the motherboard BIOS by pressing the designated key (e.g., Del, F2) during the boot process. Verify that the system recognizes the installed components, such as the CPU, RAM, and storage devices.
- Install the operating system and necessary drivers for optimal performance. Ensure all components are recognized and functioning correctly.
- Run benchmark tests or play demanding games to stress-test the system and ensure stable performance.

If any issues arise during testing, consult the component manuals, online forums, or contact customer support for troubleshooting assistance.

Bios And Software Setup

Understanding the Basic Input/Output System (BIOS)

The Basic Input/Output System (BIOS) is firmware embedded in the motherboard of a computer. It is responsible for initializing hardware components during the boot process and providing basic system settings and configurations. Understanding the BIOS is essential for managing system parameters, optimizing performance, and troubleshooting.

The BIOS provides a user interface that allows you to access and modify various settings. This includes options for boot priority, CPU and RAM configurations, power management, and hardware monitoring. It also provides information about the installed hardware and system health status.

Accessing the BIOS typically involves pressing a specific key (e.g., Del, F2, F10) during the boot process. Consult the motherboard manual or manufacturer's website for the specific key and instructions.

Updating BIOS and Firmware

Updating the BIOS and firmware is important to ensure compatibility with new hardware, improve stability, and address security vulnerabilities. However, it should be approached with caution, as an incorrect update can cause system instability or even render the motherboard unusable.

Before updating the BIOS, research and read the release notes and instructions provided by the motherboard manufacturer. These notes outline the changes and improvements introduced in the update and any precautions or steps to follow.

To update the BIOS, typically you need to download the latest firmware from the manufacturer's website onto a USB flash drive. Then, enter the BIOS and navigate to the update section. Follow the on-screen instructions to select the firmware file from the USB drive and initiate the update process.

It's important to note that updating the BIOS carries some risk, and it should only be done if there is a specific need or issue that requires an update. If your system is running smoothly, it's generally recommended to avoid unnecessary BIOS updates.

Installing Operating System (Windows, macOS, Linux)

To start using your newly built gaming PC, you need to install an operating system (OS). The choice of OS depends on your preference and compatibility with your hardware.

For Windows, you can install the OS using a bootable USB drive or DVD. Obtain a legitimate copy of the Windows installation media and follow the prompts during the installation process. You may need to enter the product key and select the desired options, such as language, disk partitioning, and user account setup.

For macOS, you can install the OS using a bootable USB drive. Download the macOS installation file from the App Store or the Apple website. Use a tool like Disk Utility to create a bootable USB drive, then follow the instructions during installation.

For Linux, there are numerous distributions available,

each with its own installation process. Choose a Linux distribution that suits your needs, download the installation ISO file, create a bootable USB drive, and follow the installation steps provided by the distribution.

During the installation process, you may need to format and partition the storage devices, create user accounts, and configure network settings. Follow the on-screen instructions and refer to the respective operating system's documentation for guidance.

Device Drivers and Software Updates

After installing the operating system, it's important to install the necessary device drivers for optimal hardware functionality. Device drivers are software programs that allow the OS to communicate with specific hardware components.

Typically, drivers for components such as the GPU, motherboard, network adapters, and audio devices are provided by the respective manufacturers. Visit their websites to download the latest drivers for your specific hardware.

It's also essential to regularly update drivers and software to ensure compatibility, performance improvements, and security patches. Manufacturers release driver updates periodically to address bugs, enhance functionality, and optimize performance. Check for updates regularly or enable automatic updates when available.

In addition to device drivers, it's important to keep the operating system itself updated with the latest patches and security updates. Most operating systems provide options for automatic updates to ensure you have the latest software improvements and security patches.

Configuring Graphics Settings and Performance Optimization

Once the operating system and drivers are installed, you can optimize your gaming PC's graphics settings to achieve the desired performance and visual quality in games.

For NVIDIA graphics cards, you can access the NVIDIA Control Panel or NVIDIA GeForce Experience software to adjust various graphics settings. These settings include resolution, refresh rate, anti-aliasing, texture filtering, and vertical sync. You can also enable features like NVIDIA G-SYNC or AMD FreeSync for smoother gameplay.

For AMD graphics cards, you can use the AMD Radeon Software to configure graphics settings. Similar to NVIDIA, you can adjust resolution, refresh rate, anti-aliasing, and other visual enhancements.

In addition to graphics settings, you can use third-party software like MSI Afterburner or EVGA Precision X1 to overclock your GPU for additional performance gains. However, overclocking should be done with caution, as it can increase power consumption and heat output.

To optimize overall performance, ensure that your system is regularly maintained. This includes cleaning dust from fans and heatsinks, managing background processes and startup applications, and periodically defragmenting or optimizing storage drives.

By configuring graphics settings and optimizing performance, you can tailor your gaming experience to achieve the desired balance between visual quality and smooth gameplay. Experiment with different settings to find the optimal configuration for each game and your specific hardware capabilities.

Customization And Upgrades

Adding RGB Lighting and Aesthetic Enhancements

Adding RGB lighting and other aesthetic enhancements can personalize and enhance the visual appeal of your gaming PC. Here are some options to consider:

- RGB Fans: Replace standard case fans with RGB fans to add vibrant lighting effects and improve airflow. These fans often come with customizable lighting options and can be synchronized with other RGB components.
- RGB LED Strips: Attach RGB LED strips inside the case to illuminate the interior and create an ambient glow. These strips can be easily installed using adhesive backing and controlled through software or physical controllers.
- RGB CPU Coolers: Upgrade your CPU cooler to one that incorporates RGB lighting. This adds visual flair to the cooling system and enhances the overall aesthetics of the build.
- RGB RAM: Consider purchasing RAM modules that feature RGB lighting. These modules often have customizable lighting effects and can sync with other RGB components for a cohesive look.
- RGB Power Supply: Some power supply units offer RGB lighting options, allowing you to add visual flair to an otherwise overlooked component.

Remember to ensure that the RGB components you choose are compatible with your motherboard's RGB header or have their own independent lighting control software.

Upgrading Components over Time

One of the advantages of building your own gaming PC is the flexibility to upgrade components over time. As technology advances and your needs evolve, you can enhance your system's performance by upgrading specific parts. Here are some common components that can be upgraded:

- GPU: Upgrading the graphics card can have a significant impact on gaming performance, allowing you to play the latest games at higher resolutions and settings.
- CPU: Upgrading the CPU can improve processing power and overall system responsiveness. This is particularly beneficial for CPU-intensive tasks such as content creation or streaming.
- RAM: Adding more RAM or upgrading to faster modules can enhance multitasking capabilities and improve performance in memory-intensive applications.
- Storage: Upgrading storage drives, such as replacing an HDD with an SSD or upgrading to a faster NVMe drive, can significantly reduce loading times and improve overall system responsiveness.
- PSU: Upgrading to a higher wattage or more efficient power supply unit can accommodate power-hungry components and improve energy efficiency.

When upgrading components, consider compatibility with existing hardware and ensure that your power supply can handle the increased power requirements. It's also important to research and compare different models to choose components that offer the best value for your specific needs.

Overclocking and Performance Tweaking

Overclocking refers to running a component, such as the CPU or GPU, at higher speeds than its stock settings to achieve increased performance. While overclocking can provide performance gains, it also increases power consumption and generates more heat. Here are some considerations:

- CPU Overclocking: Increasing the clock speed of the CPU can boost overall system performance. This involves adjusting the CPU multiplier and voltage settings in the BIOS. However, overclocking should be done cautiously, as it can lead to instability if not properly managed.
- GPU Overclocking: Similar to CPU overclocking, increasing the clock speed of the GPU can result in better gaming performance. Tools such as MSI Afterburner or EVGA Precision X1 can be used to adjust GPU core and memory clocks. Monitor temperatures and stability during the process.
- Cooling: Overclocking generates additional heat, so adequate cooling is crucial to maintain stability and prevent damage to components. Ensure proper airflow, consider upgrading CPU and GPU coolers, and monitor temperatures using software utilities or hardware monitoring tools.
- Stress Testing: After overclocking, stress testing is essential to check system stability and ensure that temperatures are within safe limits. Use stress

testing tools like Prime95 or AIDA64 for the CPU and benchmarking software like 3DMark for the GPU.

- Incremental Overclocking: When overclocking, make small adjustments at a time and test for stability before moving on to higher settings. This allows you to find the maximum stable overclock without pushing the component too far.

It's important to note that overclocking can void warranties and may have potential risks if not done properly. It requires careful research, patience, and a good understanding of the specific component's capabilities and limitations.

CHAPTER THREE

Maintenance and
Troubleshooting

Cleaning and Dust Management

Regular cleaning and dust management are essential for maintaining optimal performance and longevity of your gaming PC. Dust accumulation can restrict airflow, cause overheating, and impact system stability. Here are some tips for cleaning and dust management:

- Dusting: Use compressed air or a can of compressed air to blow away dust from components, fans, and heatsinks. Ensure that you hold fans in place while cleaning to prevent them from spinning too fast and potentially damaging the bearings.
- Filters: Check if your PC case has dust filters on intake fans. Clean or replace these filters regularly to prevent dust from entering the system.
- Cable Management: Neatly organize cables and tie them together using cable ties or Velcro straps. This helps maintain good airflow and makes cleaning more accessible.
- Case Maintenance: Regularly wipe the exterior of the PC case with a microfiber cloth or an anti-

static cloth to remove dust and fingerprints.

- Room Environment: Keep your gaming PC in a clean and dust-free environment. Avoid placing it on the floor or in areas prone to excessive dust accumulation.

Monitoring System Health

Monitoring the health of your gaming PC allows you to identify potential issues, track system temperatures, and ensure optimal performance. Here are some ways to monitor system health:

- Temperature Monitoring: Use software utilities like HWMonitor, Core Temp, or SpeedFan to monitor CPU and GPU temperatures. High temperatures may indicate inadequate cooling or the need for dust cleaning.
- Fan Speed Monitoring: Monitor fan speeds using software or motherboard utilities. Abnormally low or fluctuating fan speeds may indicate fan malfunctions or airflow obstructions.
- Performance Monitoring: Utilize software like MSI Afterburner or HWiNFO to monitor system performance metrics such as CPU and GPU usage, clock speeds, and memory usage.
- Hardware Monitoring: Some motherboards come with built-in monitoring features. Check the manufacturer's software or BIOS for system health information, such as voltage levels and fan speeds.
- SMART Monitoring: Use SMART (Self-Monitoring, Analysis, and Reporting Technology) tools to monitor the health of your storage drives.

Software like CrystalDiskInfo can provide insights into drive health and potential failures.

Common Hardware and Software Issues

Gaming PCs may encounter hardware or software issues from time to time. Here are some common issues and their possible causes:

- Blue Screen of Death (BSOD): This error typically occurs due to faulty hardware drivers, incompatible software, or hardware issues such as RAM or storage problems.
- Game Crashes: Game crashes can be caused by outdated GPU drivers, overheating, or incompatible software. Ensure that your GPU drivers are up to date and monitor system temperatures.
- Slow Performance: Slow performance can result from inadequate RAM, fragmented storage drives, or malware infections. Upgrade RAM if necessary, regularly defragment storage drives, and run antivirus scans.
- No Power or Boot Issues: Problems with power supply connections, faulty power cables, or motherboard issues can prevent the system from powering on. Ensure all connections are secure and check for faulty components.
- Connectivity Issues: Network connectivity problems can arise due to driver issues, faulty network adapters, or router configurations. Check for updated network drivers and troubleshoot router settings if needed.

Troubleshooting Techniques and Resources

When encountering issues with your gaming PC, it's important to have troubleshooting techniques and resources at your disposal. Here are some steps to follow:

- Research: Utilize online forums, tech support websites, and manufacturer's support resources to find solutions to specific issues. Often, someone has encountered a similar problem and found a solution.
- Update Drivers and Software: Ensure that all drivers and software are up to date. Check the manufacturer's websites for the latest updates and bug fixes.
- Rollback Changes: If you recently made hardware or software changes before the issue occurred, try rolling back those changes to see if the problem resolves.
- Test Hardware: Run diagnostic tests on individual hardware components, such as RAM, storage drives, and GPU, to identify any potential issues. Tools like Memtest86, manufacturer-provided diagnostic software, or benchmarking utilities can help.
- Clean Reinstallation: If software issues persist, consider performing a clean reinstallation of the operating system to eliminate any underlying software conflicts.
- Seek Professional Help: If you are unable to resolve the issue on your own, consider seeking assistance from a professional technician or contacting the manufacturer's customer support for further guidance.

By following these troubleshooting techniques and utilizing available resources, you can effectively diagnose and resolve hardware and software issues with your gaming PC.

Networking And Online Gaming

Understanding Network Hardware (Routers, Modems, etc.)

When it comes to setting up a reliable and efficient network for gaming, understanding the various network hardware components is crucial. Here are some key components:

- Modem: A modem is the device that connects your home network to your internet service provider (ISP). It converts the incoming signal from your ISP into a form that can be used by your network devices.
- Router: A router is responsible for directing network traffic between devices in your home network and managing connections between your local network and the internet. It allows multiple devices to connect to the internet simultaneously and provides features like Wi-Fi connectivity, network security, and port forwarding.
- Switch: A switch is used to expand the number of Ethernet ports available on your network. It allows you to connect multiple devices using wired Ethernet connections for faster and more stable connections compared to Wi-Fi.
- Access Point: An access point (AP) is used to extend the coverage of your Wi-Fi network. It is useful for larger homes or areas where the router's Wi-Fi signal may not reach. Access points connect to the router via a wired connection and provide additional Wi-Fi coverage.

- Network Extender: Similar to an access point, a network extender is used to extend the coverage of your Wi-Fi network. However, network extenders create a separate network and can result in reduced network speeds compared to access points.

Internet Connection Types and Speeds

Internet connection types and speeds vary depending on your location and service provider. Here are some common internet connection types:

- Digital Subscriber Line (DSL): DSL uses existing telephone lines to provide internet connectivity. Speeds can range from a few megabits per second (Mbps) to several hundred Mbps depending on the distance from the telephone exchange.
- Cable Internet: Cable internet utilizes the same coaxial cable infrastructure as cable TV. It offers higher speeds compared to DSL and can range from tens to hundreds of Mbps.
- Fiber Optic: Fiber optic connections use light signals transmitted through thin glass fibers. Fiber connections offer the highest speeds, ranging from hundreds of Mbps to multiple gigabits per second (Gbps).
- Satellite Internet: Satellite internet is available in areas where wired connections are not feasible. It provides internet connectivity via satellite signals but can have higher latency and limited speeds compared to wired connections.
- Mobile Broadband: Mobile broadband uses cellular networks to provide internet connectivity. Speeds

can vary depending on the network coverage and technology (3G, 4G, 5G) available in your area.

To determine the speed of your internet connection, you can use online speed testing tools. Keep in mind that the advertised speed by your ISP may not always match the actual speeds you experience, as they can be influenced by factors such as network congestion and distance from the service provider's infrastructure.

Optimizing Network Settings for Gaming

Optimizing network settings can help reduce latency, ensure a stable connection, and enhance the gaming experience. Here are some tips to optimize your network settings for gaming:

- Wired Connection: Whenever possible, use a wired Ethernet connection instead of Wi-Fi. Wired connections provide more stability and lower latency, resulting in a smoother gaming experience.
- Quality of Service (QoS): Many routers have QoS settings that allow you to prioritize gaming traffic over other network activities. This ensures that gaming data receives higher priority, reducing the impact of other network traffic on latency and stability.
- Port Forwarding: If you experience connectivity issues or problems with specific games, port forwarding can help. It allows incoming traffic to bypass certain network restrictions, improving connection reliability. Consult the game's documentation or online resources for specific port forwarding instructions.

- DNS Settings: Changing your DNS (Domain Name System) settings to a more reliable or faster DNS server can improve website loading times and reduce latency. Public DNS servers like Google DNS or Cloudflare DNS are commonly recommended.
- Bandwidth Management: Limit or manage bandwidth-intensive applications and downloads when gaming. This ensures that gaming traffic has sufficient bandwidth for optimal performance.
- Firmware Updates: Keep your router's firmware up to date. Router manufacturers often release firmware updates that address security vulnerabilities, improve stability, and enhance performance.
- Close Background Applications: Close or limit background applications and downloads that consume network resources. This helps reduce network congestion and frees up bandwidth for gaming.

Online Security and Privacy Considerations

When gaming online, it's essential to consider online security and privacy to protect your personal information and ensure a safe gaming experience. Here are some considerations:

- Firewall: Enable a firewall on your router and PC to protect against unauthorized access and malicious activities.
- Antivirus Software: Install reputable antivirus software and keep it updated to protect against malware and other security threats.

- Secure Wi-Fi: Use a strong, unique password for your Wi-Fi network to prevent unauthorized access. Consider using WPA2 or WPA3 encryption for enhanced security.
- Strong Passwords: Use strong, unique passwords for your gaming accounts and enable two-factor authentication (2FA) whenever possible.
- Game Updates: Keep your games and gaming platforms up to date by installing the latest patches and updates. This helps protect against security vulnerabilities.
- Be Cautious of Scams: Be wary of phishing attempts, suspicious links, or downloads from untrusted sources. Avoid sharing personal information with unknown individuals or websites.
- Gaming Privacy Settings: Review and adjust privacy settings within gaming platforms to control what information is shared publicly or with other players.
- Virtual Private Network (VPN): Consider using a VPN for an added layer of security and privacy. VPNs encrypt your internet traffic and can help protect your identity and data.

By considering these security and privacy measures, you can enjoy online gaming with peace of mind, knowing that your personal information is protected and your gaming experience is secure.

Advanced Topics

Virtual Reality (VR) Gaming

Virtual Reality (VR) gaming offers an immersive and interactive gaming experience. It involves the use of a VR headset and controllers to transport players into a virtual environment. Here are some key aspects of VR gaming:

- VR Headsets: VR headsets are the primary hardware used in VR gaming. They typically consist of a high-resolution display, motion sensors, and audio. Popular VR headset brands include Oculus, HTC Vive, and PlayStation VR.
- System Requirements: VR gaming requires a powerful gaming PC capable of handling the demands of rendering VR environments. Check the specific requirements of the VR headset and games to ensure compatibility with your PC.
- VR Controllers: VR controllers allow players to interact with the virtual environment. They typically feature motion tracking, buttons, and triggers to replicate hand movements and gestures in the virtual world.
- VR Gaming Experiences: VR gaming offers a wide range of experiences, from action-packed shooters to immersive exploration games. Some games are specifically designed for VR, while others offer VR support as an additional feature.
- Room-scale VR: Room-scale VR allows players to move around a designated play area, providing a more immersive experience. This requires sufficient space and tracking devices to detect the

player's movement.

- Motion Sickness: Some individuals may experience motion sickness or discomfort when playing VR games due to the disconnect between visual cues and physical movements. Start with shorter gaming sessions and gradually increase the duration to build tolerance.
- VR Content: Aside from gaming, VR technology is also used for various other applications, including educational experiences, virtual tours, and creative tools for artists and designers.

Multi-Monitor Setup and Eyefinity

A multi-monitor setup and Eyefinity technology can enhance the gaming experience by expanding the display area and creating a wider field of view. Here's what you need to know:

- Multi-Monitor Setup: A multi-monitor setup involves connecting two or more monitors to your gaming PC. This allows you to have a larger desktop workspace and provides a wider display area for gaming.
- Eyefinity: Eyefinity is a technology developed by AMD that enables seamless gaming across multiple monitors. It allows you to combine the displays into a single extended desktop, creating a panoramic view.
- System Requirements: To set up a multi-monitor configuration, ensure that your graphics card supports multiple displays and has sufficient video outputs. Most modern graphics cards can handle multiple monitors, but it's essential to

check the specifications.

- Display Arrangement: In a multi-monitor setup, you can arrange the displays in different configurations, such as side by side, stacked, or angled. Adjust the positioning and orientation based on your preference and the physical layout of your workspace.
- Bezel Correction: Bezels (the frames around each monitor) can interrupt the seamless experience in multi-monitor gaming. Some graphics card software allows you to apply bezel correction, reducing the visual impact of bezels on the screen.
- Game Support: Not all games fully support multi-monitor setups. Some games may require manual adjustments or third-party software to span across multiple displays. Check the game's settings or online resources for instructions on enabling multi-monitor support.
- Performance Considerations: Running games across multiple monitors can increase the graphical demands on your system. Ensure that your gaming PC meets the recommended specifications for multi-monitor gaming to maintain smooth performance.

Building a Home Media Server

Building a home media server allows you to centralize and access your media content, such as movies, TV shows, music, and photos, from various devices within your home network. Here's what you need to know:

- Hardware Requirements: To build a home media server, you'll need a computer or a dedicated server capable of storing and serving your media files. Consider the storage capacity, processing power, and network connectivity of the server.

- Operating System: Choose an operating system suitable for your needs and preferences. Popular options for home media servers include Windows Home Server, FreeNAS, or Linux-based solutions like Ubuntu Server or CentOS.
- Storage: Determine the amount of storage space required to accommodate your media files. Consider using multiple hard drives, RAID configurations, or network-attached storage (NAS) solutions for added redundancy and scalability.
- Media Server Software: Install media server software to manage and stream your media content. Popular options include Plex, Emby, and Kodi. These software solutions offer features like media organization, transcoding, and remote access.
- Media Streaming Devices: To access media from your home media server, you'll need media streaming devices connected to your TVs or other playback devices. Options include streaming boxes (e.g., Roku, Apple TV) or smart TVs with built-in streaming capabilities.
- Network Setup: Ensure your home network is properly configured for streaming media. Use wired connections when possible for optimal performance, especially when streaming high-definition content.
- Organization and Metadata: Properly organize your media files and use metadata tools provided

by media server software to enhance the browsing experience. This includes retrieving cover art, descriptions, and other information for your media.

- Remote Access: Many media server solutions offer remote access capabilities, allowing you to stream your media content outside of your home network. Configure remote access securely to protect your privacy and data.

Streaming and Content Creation

Streaming and content creation have become popular activities among gamers and creators alike. Here's what you need to know about these areas:

- Streaming: Streaming allows you to broadcast your gameplay or content live over the internet. Platforms like Twitch, YouTube Live, and Facebook Gaming are commonly used for streaming.
- Streaming Software: To stream, you'll need streaming software, also known as broadcasting software or encoding software. Popular options include OBS Studio, Streamlabs OBS, and XSplit. These software solutions enable you to capture your gameplay, overlay graphics, and stream to the chosen platform.
- Internet Connection: A stable and high-speed internet connection is essential for streaming. Ensure that your upload speed meets the requirements of the streaming platform and that you have sufficient bandwidth for a smooth streaming experience.

- Content Creation: Content creation involves producing and sharing various forms of media, including videos, podcasts, or written content related to gaming or other topics of interest. This can be done through platforms like YouTube, TikTok, or personal websites.
- Video Editing Software: For content creation, you may need video editing software to edit and enhance your recorded gameplay or other video content. Popular options include Adobe Premiere Pro, Final Cut Pro, and Davinci Resolve.
- Microphones and Cameras: Depending on the type of content you create, you may need a microphone for clear audio recording and a camera for facecam or vlog-style content. USB microphones like the Blue Yeti and webcams like the Logitech C920 are commonly used options.
- Content Creation Tools: Explore additional tools and resources to enhance your content, such as graphic design software (e.g., Adobe Photoshop, Canva), audio editing software (e.g., Audacity, Adobe Audition), or thumbnail creation tools.
- Engagement and Community Building: Building an audience and engaging with your viewers or readers is crucial for success in streaming and content creation. Interact with your community through chat, comments, social media, and consider establishing a consistent streaming or content release schedule.

Remember to research and adhere to platform guidelines and copyright laws when streaming or creating content. Building a dedicated and engaged community takes time and consistency, so be patient and enjoy the creative process.

Gaming Pc Maintenance And Upgrades Timeline

Recommended Maintenance Schedule

Regular maintenance is essential to keep your gaming PC running smoothly and to prolong its lifespan. Here's a recommended maintenance schedule:

Daily:

- Clean the PC case exterior using a microfiber cloth to remove dust and fingerprints.
- Check for any unusual noises or vibrations during operation.

Weekly:

- Dust the PC case interior using compressed air or a can of compressed air to remove accumulated dust from components, fans, and heatsinks.
- Check the cable connections to ensure they are secure.

Monthly:

- Clean the monitor(s) using a microfiber cloth and appropriate cleaning solution.
- Check and clean the keyboard and mouse to remove dirt and debris.

Every 3-6 Months:

- Clean the PC case fans and heatsinks more thoroughly, ensuring optimal airflow.
- Check for any signs of capacitor bulging or leaking on the motherboard and other components.
- Update software and drivers, including operating

system updates and the latest drivers for components.

Every 6-12 Months:

- Remove and clean the CPU cooler, reapplying thermal paste if necessary.
- Check the status of storage drives and perform disk cleanup or defragmentation if needed.
- Evaluate the system's performance and consider upgrading components if required for improved gaming experience.

It's important to note that the maintenance schedule may vary depending on the specific conditions and usage of your gaming PC. Regular monitoring of temperatures, performance, and system health will help identify any maintenance needs that may arise outside of the recommended schedule.

Upgrade Paths and Future-proofing

Technology evolves rapidly, and it's important to consider upgrade paths and future-proofing when building or upgrading your gaming PC. Here are some factors to consider:

- Expansion Slots: Choose a motherboard with adequate expansion slots to accommodate future upgrades, such as additional RAM, storage, or expansion cards (e.g., sound cards, network cards).
- Power Supply: Invest in a power supply unit (PSU) with a higher wattage than your current needs to allow for future upgrades. Ensure it has the necessary connectors to support potential

upgrades.

- CPU Socket Compatibility: Select a motherboard with a CPU socket that supports the latest processors and offers a potential upgrade path. This allows you to upgrade the CPU without having to replace the entire motherboard.
- RAM Capacity: Opt for a motherboard with sufficient RAM slots and consider starting with a lower amount of RAM but leaving room for expansion. This allows you to add more RAM modules in the future as needed.
- GPU Compatibility: Choose a motherboard and power supply unit that can support high-performance graphics cards. Consider the physical dimensions and power requirements of future GPU upgrades.
- Storage Options: Plan for future storage needs by leaving room for additional storage drives or opting for a motherboard with multiple M.2 slots or SATA ports. This provides flexibility for expanding storage capacity.
- Connectivity and Future Standards: Consider future connectivity needs, such as USB 3.1 or USB-C ports, Wi-Fi 6 support, or Thunderbolt compatibility. This ensures compatibility with emerging technologies and devices.
- Research and Future Trends: Stay informed about upcoming technologies and trends in the gaming industry. This includes advancements in graphics, virtual reality, and other hardware or software innovations that may impact future upgrades.

While it's challenging to future-proof a gaming PC completely, considering these factors and staying informed about industry developments can help extend the lifespan and adaptability of your system. It's important to regularly reassess your needs and budget for upgrades accordingly to ensure a satisfying gaming experience.

CHAPTER FOUR

Troubleshooting Guide

Common Issues and Solutions

Despite the best efforts in building and maintaining a gaming PC, various issues can arise. Here are some common issues and their potential solutions:

System Crashes or Freezes:

- Ensure that your hardware components are properly seated and connected.
- Check for overheating issues by monitoring temperatures and cleaning dust from fans and heatsinks.
- Update device drivers and software to the latest versions.
- Test memory modules for errors using tools like Memtest86+.
- Scan for malware or viruses that could be causing system instability.

Blue Screen of Death (BSOD) Errors:

- Check for driver conflicts or outdated drivers. Update drivers for components such as the GPU, motherboard, and network adapters.
- Verify compatibility of hardware and software components. Incompatible hardware or software

can cause BSOD errors.

- Run a memory test to check for faulty RAM modules.
- If the issue persists, consult the error code provided by the BSOD and search for specific solutions related to that code.

Slow Performance or Lag:

- Ensure that your system meets the minimum requirements for the game or software you're using.
- Close unnecessary background applications to free up system resources.
- Check for malware or adware that may be consuming system resources.
- Optimize graphics settings in games to balance performance and visual quality.
- Run disk cleanup or defragmentation to optimize storage drive performance.

Connectivity Issues:

- Check network cables and connections to ensure they are secure.
- Restart your router and modem to refresh the connection.
- Update network drivers for your network adapter.
- Troubleshoot network settings and ensure the correct IP address configuration.
- Disable or adjust firewall and antivirus settings that may be blocking network connections.

No Display or Video Issues:

- Verify that the monitor is properly connected to the GPU and that the cables are secure.

- Ensure that the monitor is powered on and set to the correct input source.
- Check the GPU power connections to ensure proper power delivery.
- Update GPU drivers to the latest version.
- Test the monitor and cables with another known working system to rule out hardware issues.

Diagnostic Tools and Software

Diagnostic tools and software can help identify and resolve issues with your gaming PC. Here are some commonly used tools:

- CPU-Z: Provides detailed information about your CPU, motherboard, memory, and other system components.
- GPU-Z: Monitors and provides information about your GPU, including clock speeds, temperatures, and memory usage.
- HWMonitor: Monitors temperatures, voltages, and fan speeds of various components in real-time.
- Memtest86+: A memory diagnostic tool that tests RAM modules for errors and stability.
- CrystalDiskInfo: Monitors the health and status of your storage drives, providing information about SMART attributes and potential drive failures.
- Prime95: A stress-testing tool that can help identify stability issues in your CPU and system.
- FurMark: A GPU stress-testing tool that pushes your graphics card to its limits to test stability and heat output.
- Windows Event Viewer: Provides logs and error

messages that can help identify the cause of system crashes or errors.

- Performance Monitor: A built-in Windows tool that monitors system performance and generates reports for analyzing resource usage.
- Malwarebytes: An antivirus and anti-malware software that scans and removes malware infections.

These tools can assist in diagnosing hardware or software issues, monitoring system health, and troubleshooting problems with your gaming PC. However, it's important to exercise caution and follow the provided instructions when using diagnostic tools, as they can affect system stability and performance

Tips For Buying Pc Components

Researching Reliable Brands and Models

When building or purchasing components for your gaming PC, it's important to research reliable brands and models to ensure quality and reliability. Here's how to conduct research:

- Manufacturer Reputation: Research the reputation of different hardware manufacturers. Look for brands with a history of producing reliable and high-quality components.
- Online Communities and Forums: Participate in online communities and forums dedicated to gaming and PC hardware. Seek recommendations and opinions from experienced users who have firsthand experience with different brands and models.
- Professional Reviews: Read reviews from reputable technology websites and publications. These reviews often provide in-depth analysis and performance comparisons of various components.
- User Reviews: Read user reviews on retailer websites or dedicated PC hardware review platforms. User reviews can provide insights into real-world experiences with specific products.
- Consider Compatibility: Ensure that the components you choose are compatible with each other and with your intended use. Check the specifications and compatibility lists provided by manufacturers.

- Longevity and Support: Consider the longevity of a brand's product support and driver updates. Brands that offer long-term support and regular updates often provide a better user experience.
- Check for Product Recalls: Research any past recalls or known issues with specific models. This information can help you avoid potential problems with your chosen components.
- Ask for Recommendations: Seek advice from trusted friends, fellow gamers, or tech-savvy individuals who have experience with PC hardware. Their personal experiences and recommendations can be valuable in your decision-making process.

Remember that reliable brands and models can vary across different components, such as CPUs, GPUs, motherboards, and storage devices. It's important to research each component individually to ensure you make informed choices for your gaming PC.

Reading Reviews and Comparisons

Reading reviews and comparisons is a valuable step in selecting the best components for your gaming PC. Here's how to make the most of reviews and comparisons:

- Reputable Sources: Look for reviews from reputable technology websites, magazines, or publications that specialize in PC hardware. These sources often have experienced reviewers and conduct thorough testing.
- Multiple Sources: Read reviews from multiple sources to gather a range of opinions and perspectives. This helps to minimize biases and

provide a more comprehensive understanding of a product's strengths and weaknesses.

- Performance Benchmarks: Pay attention to performance benchmarks provided in reviews. Benchmarks compare the component's performance against other models and provide objective data for comparison.
- Consider Use Cases: Assess reviews that specifically address your intended use cases, such as gaming performance, content creation, or streaming. Components may perform differently depending on the specific workload.
- Real-World Experiences: Look for reviews that discuss real-world experiences and considerations like noise levels, temperatures, and build quality. These factors may be important depending on your preferences and environment.
- Comparisons and Roundups: Read comparisons and roundups that evaluate multiple models within a specific component category. These articles can provide a side-by-side analysis, making it easier to compare features, performance, and value.
- User Reviews: While professional reviews are valuable, also consider reading user reviews on retailer websites. User reviews offer insights into long-term usage, reliability, and potential issues that may not be immediately apparent.
- Critical Evaluation: Be critical of reviews and consider the reviewer's biases, methodology, and any potential conflicts of interest. Look for consistency in opinions across multiple reviews.

Understanding Warranties and Return Policies

Understanding warranties and return policies is crucial when purchasing components for your gaming PC. Here's what to consider:

- Manufacturer's Warranty: Check the manufacturer's warranty for each component. Warranties can vary in duration, coverage, and conditions. Ensure you understand the terms and any restrictions, such as voiding the warranty by overclocking or using incompatible components.
- Extended Warranties: Some retailers offer extended warranties for an additional fee. Evaluate the value of extended warranties based on the cost of the component, its expected lifespan, and the likelihood of needing repairs or replacements.
- Return Policies: Familiarize yourself with the retailer's return policies. Understand the conditions for returning or exchanging components, including time limits, restocking fees, and whether opened products can be returned.
- Compatibility Guarantee: Some retailers or manufacturers offer compatibility guarantees, ensuring that the purchased components will work together. This can provide peace of mind when building a gaming PC.
- Customer Support: Research the customer support reputation of the manufacturer or retailer. Prompt and helpful customer support can be crucial if you encounter any issues or have questions about the product.

- Verified Retailers: Purchase components from verified and reputable retailers. Check customer reviews and ratings to ensure a positive buying experience and reliable customer support.
- Product Registration: Register your components with the manufacturer if required. Registration can provide access to additional support, firmware updates, and notifications about potential recalls or issues.
- Keep Documentation: Keep all receipts, warranties, and documentation related to your purchased components. This will be helpful if you need to file a warranty claim or return a product.

Understanding warranties and return policies provides you with protection and recourse in case of faulty or incompatible components. Take the time to read and comprehend the terms and conditions to make informed decisions and ensure a smooth purchasing experience.

CONCLUSION

In conclusion, building your own gaming PC can be an immensely rewarding and exciting journey. Throughout this guide, we have explored the various components, considerations, and step-by-step processes involved in creating a powerful and personalized gaming rig. By following these principles and guidelines, you have equipped yourself with the knowledge and confidence to embark on your own PC-building adventure.

Building a gaming PC offers numerous benefits, including cost-effectiveness, customization options, and the opportunity to gain a deeper understanding of computer hardware. It allows you to tailor your system to your specific gaming needs, ensuring optimal performance and the ability to play the latest titles at their highest settings.

Remember that patience and thoroughness are key when assembling your gaming PC. Take the time to research, compare, and select the best components that fit within your budget and desired specifications. Keep in mind that technology is ever-evolving, and it's important to stay updated on the latest advancements and trends in the gaming industry.

Furthermore, building a PC is not just a one-time endeavor but an ongoing process. As you delve into the world of PC gaming, you may find yourself upgrading components, tweaking settings, and exploring new possibilities.

Embrace this continuous learning experience, as it will only enhance your gaming performance and overall enjoyment.

Finally, don't forget to share your knowledge and experiences with others. The PC-building community is vast and supportive, with numerous forums, online communities, and resources available. By engaging with fellow enthusiasts, you can expand your understanding, gather valuable insights, and contribute to the collective knowledge of PC gaming.

So, take hold of your screwdriver, unleash your creativity, and embark on your journey to build the ultimate gaming PC. May your gaming experiences be immersive, your framerates high, and your victories legendary. Happy building!

www.ingramcontent.com/pod-product-compliance
Lightning Source LLC
LaVergne TN
LVHW051749050326
832903LV00029B/2801